About the Author

Paul Lawless is retired and lives in Sheffield surrounded by family and friends.

To Tom e Virginia

With best wishes

Paul X

A Late Journey

Paul Lawless

A Late Journey

Olympia Publishers
London

www.olympiapublishers.com
OLYMPIA PAPERBACK EDITION

A CIP catalogue record for this title is
available from the British Library.

ISBN: 978-1-80074-986-3

First Published in 2023

Olympia Publishers
Tallis House
2 Tallis Street
London
EC4Y 0AB

Printed in Great Britain

Dedication

To the memory of Mary Lawless (1949–2020)

Acknowledgements

I began to write this collection of poems early in 2021, at a time of considerable personal turmoil. Mary had been dead for a year, and other things were happening in my world, many, but not all, of which are explored in this book. I remember walking in the local park thinking I needed to do something, I needed to respond to this grief. And it just hit me: I had to get something down on paper, a theme developed in 'Love Alone Remains'.

So I bought a notepad at the Post Office, came home, sharpened pencils, and just started – the very first phrase being "vine-latticed light" in 'Islands'; the last, written in January 2022, "can I introduce, the New Year" finishes 'Year End'. Somehow or other the bits in-between were written – I often wonder quite when and how that all happened. But it did, and along the way, that overpowering grief began to fade and then it just fell off me. I doubt writing of itself cracked it, but equally so I am sure it helped. Writing as therapy? It might catch on.

Thanks first to Olympia Publishers for agreeing to publish this collection. After Mary became more seriously ill in 2019, the close family formed what has proved to be the most fantastic of informal self-help groups. I cannot thank them enough for supporting me during this most difficult of times: Anna, Ruth, Jim and Paddy. My three grandchildren,

Lila, Frankie and Joe, have been wonderful at bringing me down to earth, increasingly often, quite literally. Thanks to so many people who supported the two of us before Mary's death in February 2020, and me since.

I would like to mention Tina Beatty, Peter Wells, Lu South, Jim Flannery, Pete Alcock, Kieran Hickey, Sue and Colin Smith, Liz and John Illman, Tony and Carole Bennett, Sally and Peter Jones, Richard and Di Melvin, Carolyn Bealby, Cath Cairns, Chris Evans, Viv Esberger, Frank Brown, Marlene Howarth, Ged and Vron Lawless, Dave and Doreen Smillie, Val and Martin Ross, and Nik and Tricia Goffin. Thanks to you all. Particular thanks are due to Wendy and Jerry Wellington staunch friends; Bob Bealby for wise advice, especially around the time of Mary's funeral; John Howarth, 'dearest and oldest' of friends; and Ian Cole, friend and colleague for more than thirty years. He was the first to read a half-finished version, and whilst he didn't exactly say rush home now and finish it, he didn't either say stop immediately – so I carried on. We can all blame him.
Paul Lawless, Sheffield, February 2022.

Loving

Festival

London beckoned.
I had been before
years earlier, with family, often as a student.
Most memorably: only sixteen,
recurring image still,
staying with friend's sister,
brief staging post on pilgrimage south.
Sixty years later I recall, I can taste,
that overwhelming sense of excitement,
as our host, Pied-Piper-like,
corralling acquaintances en route,
ushered us along sun-drenched, music-filled streets,
to sit, jazz serenaded,
in a Victorian pub garden.
By far the youngest, I sat in awe,
studying the easy, inclusive grace
of those accommodating souls.
Most dead now, I suppose – certainly, she is.
Soon after, I discovered this young,
auburn-haired charmer
was even then nursing a tumour,
shortly to kill her.
Cancer has befriended my journey.

Nearly a decade on, living there: that felt different.
Hard to recall, but London could be so cruel.
Fresh from failed relationship, tied to tedious tasks,
distanced from capital friends,
I felt abandoned; lowest of all,
flat mates absent, alone,
one long weekend, religious holiday,
pacing empty, wet streets
of a deserted northern suburb.

Then that golden city on the hill spread its magic.
As each generation discovers, London gives:
that sense of being, of excitement,
a wild vortex of vitality,
a pleasure dome round every corner.
Everywhere a blossoming of women:
enticing, alluring, available.
Nurtured in cold-cloistered scholarship,
this felt, smelt, very different.
There were so many.
Where did I meet them?
Work, I suppose, friends;
there were always parties.
Most now forgotten.
Odd to think I once knew these women,
enjoyed their company,
foolishly thought I loved a few.
But they slipped away.
There must have come a time
when one of us simply drifted off.
People did. There were always others,

each slightly shameful abandonment
shrouded in London's greatest gift:
anonymity.
I still recall some:
tiny Chinese girl distraught from family murder;
stunning, over-protective, Italian girl;
colleague admitting love on her wedding eve;
suburban girl eager to capture a university type;
a glittering, paranoid, orphan.
They taught me things, those capital girls.
I came to love the company of women,
momentous transformation
for one reared in masculine haunts.
Our lives are splintered by revelation,
here was the biggest of all:
women were as interested in me as I in them.

Now, such an achingly long time ago,
it is not faces that linger, but places.
Soho, Limehouse, the river at Chiswick,
the Heath, Blackfriars, Islington,
Highgate, Hammersmith:
just reciting these names shakes me even now.
Not because of what they were,
but because – unrealised then –
this was to be the very best of times:
we had youth with us.
And the pubs,
hidden, accommodating, shimmering,
brilliant white grottos in red suburbs.
Would we meet at the Princess Louise,

The Knights of St John,
perhaps the Prospect of Whitby,
or, most exotic of all,
The Mayflower?
Members of a secret society, we would plan,
decide, magically converge, renewing eternal vows.
Now, of all those elect, I see just two:
friendships forged in certainty of youth,
crumbling in time's destructive grasp.

Paths taken, doors sliding,
one festival was to change
everything.
Fresh from lunchtime pub banter,
in a nurse-filled kitchen,
boisterously jockeying for beer,
priming post-match revelry,
a drunken call to arms, we,
eager to catch the game,
careered, fawn-like, giggling
down a slippery corridor,
purple-doored, defended lounge,
to find, bursting through,
sitting there, solitary and serene,
a hazel-eyed, raven-haired
beauty.

Opposite, Facing

Our solitary beauty fled,
returning hours later,
we intruders ever more entrenched.
Game as ever, she joined in,
shared flats allowing no privacy I was delighted to see.
We chatted. There was a grace,
a charm, an elegance, about her; a cautious reserve too.
Alcohol emboldened, I asked if she enjoyed the theatre –
a usually successful, apparently innocent, ploy.
She did. We saw Olivier the following week.
Crab-like, we skirted around each other,
until, trembling at the deed, my invitation:
a weekend under canvas in Yorkshire,
an unromantic notion even then.

On a glorious, sweltering evening,
we wandered through a lupin-laden pub garden,
past tabled drinkers, around burning hearth,
between white, hewn walls,
to dance unseen on a streamside,
oak bedecked terrace.
Something happened to me – to us – that night.
I had admired others,
but this aching turmoil, this vortex of passion,
this utterly encircling shroud of love,

burnished an emotional intensity
I had never before remotely encountered,
nor was to do so again until after her death.

Weeks later in that most brilliant of summers,
we sat alone in the heart of a sweltering,
barren Regents Park,
so bereft of life, we could have been looking
into an Utrillo painting.
Holding hands, we came to an agreement
to endure forty-five years.

A distant vision warms still:
Saturday in that glorious season,
Heath meeting of friends, coffee, lunch,
neglected court, weed choked,
broken nets, lost lines,
old wooden rackets, dead balls,
giggling play, a close set,
switching of partners;
not at shoulder, beside,
but opposite, facing.

A Compassionate Woman

A mundane, suburban childhood;
a gregarious father, unknown to me;
widowed with young children, half-sisters;
remarried to a brooding, paranoid, Irish Catholic.
Catholicism haunted our lives.
My narrative was simple.
Brought up in the faith, schooled in its colleges,
I had no truck with its scented hypocrisies.
Her mother – always suspicious of me,
preferring the thought of gingered,
Irish medics, to fulfil role of son-in-law –
called me apostate.
Hers always more nuanced a stand:
there was a spiritual side to her,
nurtured by easing so many over the line.
She knew, had seen so often, the transience of being,
seen so many cross that floating frontier,
between life and death.
She had witnessed too, the mystifying power of healing,
driven not by drugs, but touch.
Through distant friends we knew a healer,
a rich man, no charlatan, granted unearthly powers to heal:
at the hospice glancing touches shattering a glass table.
I remained sceptical, preferring powers of chemistry;
but saw something of what inspired her, when, after surgery,

a gifted friend placed hands on my knee:
a quite bewildering shock of relief.
She was always to believe in other things,
other worlds, the irrational, the impermanent,
a sense that the dead do not entirely leave us.

How can unions last so long?
Those joined early in life,
have little sense of what will come,
nothing of journeys made by partners.
We changed as all do; luck was with us.
We moved the same way: more modest, quieter,
able to live with quirks and foibles,
most vital of all: granting space.
Luck came to our rescue again, when,
years into marriage, for the only time,
and at the same time,
other people came into our lives.
I pondered briefly on another path,
suspect she may have done;
it all came to nothing,
uncertain gain no match for known loss.

She adored children, ours and the later generation.
I treasure a photo, the first with first born,
a benign pieta: face transfixed with joy
an all-encompassing love for this strange new being,
serene, complete, composed.
Man of my generation, I found babies trying:
an interruption to normality.
I recall friends, newly blessed, convinced

nothing would change – a forlorn hope.
She taught me to enjoy these beings,
to revel in their existence, their exotic lives:
they would become part of us;
we should make the most of them.
She showed me patience,
knowing when to roll, fight, bargain, surrender.
Age makes certainties less secure, but one stands larger:
an intentionally childless life is a strange path to take.

Compassion ruled her.
Dying, she told me her life had been
driven by caring for others,
dedicated to lessening pain, soothing grief.
She started young; trained in medieval cloisters,
early opting for most harrowing of tasks.
She talked then of heroic options,
invasive surgery, new drugs;
but – like others – came to see futility here:
this was not working.
Later years, decades, her tenor changed:
not false promises of implausible cures,
but hope of painless passing.
She was so good at this: a born listener,
a carer, committed, aware, a reader of illness.
But all of this came at a cost.
Immersed so long –
decades –
in grief and pain,
relentless sorrow took its toll.
I wonder too at what went before;

it took her time to tell me, months.
Living abroad, previous partner,
renowned oncologist,
died overnight in their shared bed.
Never having space to grieve,
she said, a few times, we met too soon.
I squirm at the neutrality of my reaction:
so hard to grasp the horror of it,
then so far beyond me.
Too late for her,
I understand more now.
Caught between past bereavement and easing grief,
no wonder she held this secret:
she harboured a sad soul.

Let's Dance

Mykonos figured on first trip to Greece,
party island so different to the later cherished;
young, we knew no better.
One divinely ordained day, we bussed to yellow beach,
swam, sunned, returned by boat,
loved, left a dreary room,
ate by the sea, drank cocktails.
I never loved her, anyone, more than there, then.
Beachside disco, cellar bar,
wine and cold beer,
walking back to this still-standing, smiling, figure:
blue pleated skirt, white top, red shoes,
green ring, blue bracelet, white necklace,
long pendant earrings – azured, hooping,
brown-limbed, bronzed bosom, exquisite beauty;
jet black hair, shimmering in strobe lights,
golden threads,
red lips, shining,
eyes black, glistening,
hips swaying, moving,
hands out, arms embracing, trembling,
laughing, kissing:
let's dance.

Islands

Greece seduced us.
Nearly fifty years ago, barely lovers,
we first made that remembered journey:
drab, neglected city, seedy port, bleached ships.
Overnight, transformed:
that first, unforgotten blinding explosion of
ravishing blue, fusion of sea and sky,
a passion never to leave us,
pilgrims returning to that eternal miracle.

Wariness – how to navigate this maze?
We learnt.
We knew to trust ferries, would slip round rocky headlands,
every village offer life, help always gracious.
We came to hold the smells of Greece:
in winter retreat it wasn't island sights filling our heads, but
their scents.
We wondered at riotous explosions of colour –
cyclamen, orchids, bougainvillea,
gloried in that time of softening light, easing sun,
the healing hours between beating heat
and blackest of nights.
We saw inexhaustible kindness to children,
ours and others.

We uncovered unknown sadness:
village memorials to the murdered,
underplayed relief to thousands of killed soldiers;
these islands seeped blood.
A moving collage of memories:
so many shared islands, so many years,
so much of my past, our life.
Yet some visions stay large,
fading stars on darkening canvas.

As innocents, we gravitated to the known.
First call: Naxos. First meal: at a water-lapped table.
Paros, island of windmills, our second,
sea-washed love-making outraging local peasantry.
We treasured Rhodes, and its flanking glories.
Before children, with newly-met friends,
we rode its southern quarter,
arriving, dust encrusted, at remotest of pine-hidden cafe,
beside an empty beach, feeling divinely enriched.
Months later, on a London street,
I met the woman, chatted amiably,
realising only afterwards who she was:
Greece transformed us all.

A perfect day on Samos.
Distant headland,
donkey tracks to remotest of coves,
children on an empty beach,
beneath pine trees for scent and shade,
eating at a magically convened café,
returning in early, soft evening,

an inadvertently crushed, writhing snake,
caught in rear mirrors.

Later, urge for honeypots spent,
we, alone, took to quietest of Cycladean islands.
We came to read these places,
skirting dreary ports,
seeking secret, hewn paths, always there,
celestial stairways, drawing upwards,
to shimmering white, hidden, horas.
Thirst for the remote, the neglected,
took us to Naxos-fringing treasures.
On one, seemingly alone in its depth,
we climbed to a mountain-lodged monastery,
gloried in its icons, scaled encircling crags,
walked its length on rutted tracks,
returned on the only bus,
drank cold beers by an empty harbour.

A softly-recalled Dodecanese
island, most treasured of all:
I think of it often, more now.
If I ever find the courage,
if I am ever able to sit close with memories,
if I ever go again, it will be to here.
Sandy path, scent of late afternoon,
overhead accompaniment of parent and infant eagles,
deserted, tamarisk-fringed beach in vine-latticed light,
the rawest of wine, simplest food,
she, having acquired new skills,
talking to the elderly.

Nothing we had ever seen,
compared with this primitive beauty.

Years later, I returned alone,
my treatment ending,
further rounds of hers beginning.
On discovering my solitude, hotel owner,
most humane of men,
made a cache of local herbs
for an unknown woman.
Daily across this miniature paradise,
on the last around crumbling hills,
along rocky outcrops,
descending through flower-strewn,
bird-rich, empty meadows,
to emerge onto a deserted beach.
Such a shame she isn't here.
We must come again.

Where else the reckoning?
On a previously unseen island,
its port a vision of beauty,
blue-defended, white villas
flowing, lava-like, between encircling buttressed hills,
to finest of Venetian harbours,
she began to pause, to struggle, to gasp.
Within days of our return sentence had been passed:
brief, bleak, brutal future laid out.

Eternal Crete.
Landing once in early spring,

eager to grasp again that smell,
that taste, that soft heat which had beguiled us
so many times before,
we faced, and gloried in that azure sea,
and looking behind us, saw white mountains
topped out in snow.
We explored its every sinew,
worshiped its southern shores,
land-locked, ferry-necklacing villages.
We searched every gorge, every place,
every remote café, every sandy path.
Death looming, one final trip.
An elegant port, family-run hotel.
How did those most welcoming of people
know she was so ill?
We never told them.
She must by then have radiated the grace of death.
That last day, trembling in hilly olive groves,
clinging together, speechless.
We would never return.

There are ashes to be scattered there.
I doubt I can do it, not now.
Later generations must take up that challenge,
learning, on those jewels in the sun,
to thread joy with sorrow.

Revelation

Time to decide

She, of all people knew the pain, the horrors, to come:
a determined fate.
She had seen this so often,
cared for so many, eased their passing,
railing at cancer's invidious fashion parade.
Did all of this kill her, I wonder?
Did the years of tending nurture their own insidious issue?
Only half flippantly,
she often said she too would fall victim.
Why should she be immune?
When it came: fear, deep sadness
at the inevitability of it all,
once this merciless, silent killer held out its deadly embrace.
But not surprise.
From that moment, for the few years left to us,
our lives took on a different rhythm:
insistent, intensive, inclusive.
No longer could we entertain the lie
there would be years together;
our span was to be more narrowly confined.
We must love each other,
completely.

Oncologists offered qualified mercy:
It would be years perhaps;

but few lived beyond five –
a fearfully accurate prediction.
Careful at first to keep close diagnosis,
as I was later to do,
she began to broadcast the news;
it would leak out anyway.
I doubt either were prepared,
for that torrent of sympathy which hit us:
flowers filling rooms, cards every surface.
Heartening, sobering too;
so many knew where this story was heading.
Familiar as we are with the kindness of strangers,
the indifference of friends shocked.
A handful, a few, circled round the issue,
unsure how to proceed,
deciding finally to ignore it; it might go away.
We understood. After all,
how can words assuage this news?
But unforgivable, as happened later,
to adopt silence against her death.

So it began, a near five-year existential battle.
Treatment plan – sounds so positive:
disease checked, futures planned,
something being done.
Instead, an awful reality.
Each chemo dose – there were many –
prefaced by blood tests,
some failed, postponing treatment;
suffixed by sickness, overpowering tiredness,
days of discomfort, and more.

Her condition permitted surgery,
the inelegance of debulking another
painful, only partially successful, burden.
Unscheduled admissions, she a born stoic,
as unbearable, unpredictable suffering
kicked in. To round off this litany,
an icy, country walk: a broken hip.

Yet remission is cancer's handmaiden:
for four years, between increasingly frequent relapses,
she came out of it, we went for it:
tropical islands, Aegean memories, yellow forts,
desert hideouts, Atlantic hugging trails, Palladian canals.
Between adventures, she sought out peer experience,
reviewed research, logged findings,
attended Society meetings,
faithfully recording each development,
each discovery, each new source of wisdom,
scholarship to delay her death
by not one day.

Driving north to scattered earthly treasures,
soft rain glistening on black roads,
the saddest of exchanges;
she took my hand. Nothing now was working,
this disease was moving on unhindered.
It could not be long.
We gathered on white, sculptured cliffs for a last birthday,
she, miraculously free of pain.
Images from those treasured days
are strangely haunting – I often look.

She holds a palpable serenity,
a contended grace, beyond grief.
Did she intentionally ensure we each
would share a picture with her?
I see now we all did: adults, children, families.
One final celebration with treasured friends
in long favoured restaurant.
Who there knew how ill she was?
I am now unsure I did, not really:
an unwillingness to accept.
I look twice at that group image to find her
hiding in curtained shadows, a broken face.
How did she maintain mundane conversation,
knowing this to be another ending?
The talk turned to holidays.
Some, that day, had finalised distant expeditions.
I could read her thoughts,
knew precisely what was on her mind:
measuring death, spectacularly bad timing.

Her treatment ended on a grim November morning.
How many times had we made the journey across hills
to that brutalist bastion of succour and death?
More than a hundred, certainly.
Inevitably worsening news, invariably courteous heralds.
This, the last.
The four of us gathered,
oncologist and matron virtually silent,
giving her space to decide.
They knew she would, that it would be right;
further treatment was pointless.

Her journey was ending.
As we rose to leave, we four embraced,
their care and pity shining through.
I have not seen them since.
I wonder still at their skill, their patience,
and their abiding gift: granting time to decide.
I hope soon they command better weapons.

I Am So Sorry

I wish I had kept a diary;
we occupy days,
having no other currency.
Most pass by in that relentless torrent of time,
we, afterwards, able to recall
only a tiny proportion of them.
But two of recent vintage stay with me:
the time she died,
and a shattering, dank August day.

Weeks earlier, only sibling rang:
there is a plague amongst men.
Make sure you're not amongst the afflicted,
because I am.
I prevaricated, only recently pronounced unsullied.
It runs in families doctors advised;
you talk of peeing too much. Have a rerun.
At noon a few days later, the call.
I've booked you in she said;
investigations, scans, tests, results.
Oncologist,
perfect casting as insensitive consultant,
offered no solace.
It had spread, not yet to the bones. Small comfort.
In that disturbingly ambiguous phrase:

treatable but not curable.
It will probably kill you he added,
careful to eliminate misunderstanding.

That evening, we sat in joint sorrow,
each presiding over a known fate.
We compared notes.
Not good news, we agreed,
the unspoken unsaid:
her disease was altogether more aggressive,
prognosis far more uncertain.
Yet, ever compassionate she,
knowing the shock such news invokes,
aware of my pain,
took a hand, gently stroking my arm:
my dearest, you are now a member of the club
nobody wants to join. I am so sorry.

A new, unexpected, phase of my journey:
no longer just carer and joker,
but now patient and sufferer too.
Well-oiled protocol took over:
immediate hormone treatment,
chemotherapy soon to begin.
Our natures are hardwired to forget,
I can hardly now recall
that ceaseless stream of consultations,
blood tests, infusions of poison.
But, as others have found, in this fevered state,
isolated events take on unexpected significance.
Clearest memory a septic bite:

emergency admission,
the overpowering comfort of delirium,
her frightened face.
They got me through it, of course:
standard fare to those aces.

I came to accept the calming
routine of the chemo suite:
blood tests, injections, infusions.
How many hours did we two spend there,
ministered by the blessed, but granted different fates?
My disease warranting one course;
hers several, each progressively less effective.
It's a strange and intimate act,
armchair stranded, surrounded by others,
some heartbreakingly young,
tube pierced, receiving the right amount
of the right drug, at the right time.
Dangerous too;
we saw a woman have a
death-threatening reaction.
But most of the time, a placid stillness,
silence broken by beeping machines,
rarely voices;
though one fool expressed displeasure
at a timetable allowing no release over Christmas.
Lucky man.
Completers are privileged,
allowed to ring a release signalling bell.
I declined, not seeing this as any kind of ending.

The afflicted come soon to release:
treatments might prolong life,
even offer cure, but they leave their mark.
Brightly adorned, sprightly woman gave me the news:
the side effects of treatment mimic the menopause.
Expect hot flushes, weight gain, tiredness.
Some of this, but nothing too dramatic then.
Not much now.
Coyly, she underplayed the most insidious:
your libido may drop.
It doesn't – it disappears overnight.
I am neutered, my body flush with female hormones.
I knew a much younger man,
decades dead,
unwilling to make this trade off.
Who can blame him.
It is easier in your seventies; the choice less stark:
life or libido – little debate there,
doubly so with a dying wife.
Recently, hearing my story,
perceptive counsellor weighs the emotional impact
treatment has on many men.
Yes, I remember that, I recall it now.
It is coming back, it rings bells,
hidden, forgotten. It explains a lot.

It all seemed to work.
They knew what they were doing,
these unfailingly courteous experts.
For years, the numbers went the right way;
I was well, still am.

At times I felt cheated, diagnosed with a deadly disease
leaving no calling card – mixed up test results?
I transfer from the urgent reality of oncology
to calmer reaches of urology.
Not everyone there is dying.
I come to accept this intruder.
After all, I had given it life – it is me.
In early months: daily visits to chat pages
discovering horrors unknown,
visions of a future to be faced alone.
Then wisest of entries,
old hand calming the newly diagnosed:
make the most of it. We are all different;
treatments change.
You will get over that pervasive shock of diagnosis.
You will learn to live with it. And I have.
Feared blood tests look less healthy.
But I refuse to spend what remains
worrying about tiny movements of, as yet, minute figures.
There will come a time
when I need again to seek remedy,
to return to that world,
to immerse myself in the new.
But I am not yet there.
In this industry, she knew how fickle fate could be.
For fashionable cancers, new cures,
better survival rates.
For others, like her own, little change in decades.
I'm on the lucky wing: new drugs, treatments,
though not, as yet, cures.
That will come – probably too late for me,

but you never know. Live the day.

Her diagnosis affected me far more than mine.
Because she got there first?
Her prognosis more desolate?
Or was it that insistent, angry, echoing cry:
how could fate be so cruel as to inflict,
on this of all women, such a dreadful disease?
To which there is a stark, awful answer:
why not?
However good our lives,
however much love we give,
however much charity infuses our being,
unbending edict:
no favours, no freedoms.

Hospice

She looked at me on New Year's Eve,
fitting for the end of an era.
We nodded, we knew:
time to take up that invitation to finish her days at
the hospice, long a proud place of work.
I had been before, many times:
roll call then mustered my father, two aunts, an uncle,
and more than thirty years before, best of school friends.
A wife was shortly to enlist.
Did I think she would ever return?
I'm not sure now;
perhaps I avoided the thought.
I recall, a few days later, being heartened by a chaplain
revealing many patients did, for a while, go home:
for her, a hopelessly optimistic prediction.
As ever thoughtful to reduce stress,
she'd already prepared a suitcase,
its contents poignantly repacked in coming weeks
as redundancy overcame each set of clothes.
That first evening we walked entwined,
silent, heartbroken,
through a sunken garden,
a pilgrimage never to be repeated.

So it began: forty nights

in this extraordinary beacon of humanity.
How can so many –
most young – choose to care for the terminal?
Where do they find that courage
unfailingly to dispense care and wisdom to the dying,
mature in intelligence beyond their years?
This place radiates charity and humour.
We laughed with a delightful, eccentric, resident baker,
a cleaner, whose goodness would move sinners,
children discovering hidden prizes,
owner of friendliest visiting dog.

She had always wanted to die there.
I felt guilty;
surely that sacrifice should be reserved for
this place, our haven for nearly forty years?
She was adamant: we could never match that care.
She was right; towards the end she told me
there had only ever been discomfort, never pain.
How could that be when, by then, bulging tumours
ran unchecked through her ravaged body?
Reflecting now – I often do –
on those days, weeks;
there was another reason:
she wanted to spare us indignities of dying.

Have I ever lived so vivid a time?
Visiting the dying is unlike anything else.
How to balance the mundane with the sacred?
We talked of our life together,
a partnership enduring so well, so long.

We mourners fell into a rota of visits, presents,
conversations, each family member eager to engage.
Knowing the longueurs of visiting,
she granted us all freedoms, times to reflect, recover –
in my case, to pursue new sport,
a liberty later to reap unexpected consequences.

Her life seeped away,
successively losing the ability to eat, walk,
drink and, finally, talk.
I caught her between bed and bathroom
for one final, silent embrace.
Brave friends turned up to see her, to share,
until she signalled an end,
seeking final solace from we few:
me, daughters, a partner and a son-in-law
holding our hands in silent tribute.
We had welcomed him in,
this his final gift to us.

Death imminent,
for several days one stayed overnight,
exhausted, sleep impossible,
increasingly difficult to distinguish
ever-shallower breathing
from an air bed's incessant whispers.
Weeks earlier, as if passing comment
on some abstract research programme,
she told us many terminally ill die alone,
unable accompanied to let go.
Did she know this would happen to her?

Did her spirit manufacture this passing?
At home, weary, asleep, woken at the ghostly hour,
not by adjacent mobile, but distant landline,
floundering, bouncing off furniture,
navigating in the dark,
eventually found.

After so much suffering,
I should be relieved to see her dead.
But I wasn't.
Just a sense of utter loss:
Why her? Why so soon?
We three hugged this emaciated body,
little more than a collection of shrouded bones,
placed a flower at her side,
embraced a quartet of the blessed,
and, for the last time, left.
Mid-morning, gathered in favoured café,
we passed on long-awaited message,
accepted volleys of condolence.
Her journey was over,
our descent into grief beginning.

Grief

Ceremonies

Death proved easy: custodians of grief,
all women, held my hand and
led through ceremonies.
Legion offers of accompaniment,
but it seemed fitting that
we two should together
complete these funereal tasks.
Kindly registrar dispenses certification.
Undertakers lead us through choices.
Strange that coffins, ashes, services
prove to be the last of mutual choices,
decisions made easy because she,
sparing us formalities of death,
had already bestowed assistance and instruction.
During one late hospital admission,
she recruited most generous of chaplains,
whose serenity held us steady.
A simple order of service.
Albinoni's sublime Adagio prefaced
the ceremony. A fitting choice;
it had graced our wedding, four decades earlier.
She had written, read to me,
far too modest a eulogy.
I embellished it, memorised it,
not trusting to read it through.

But could I stand there and voice
this tribute to another's life,
however dear?
Better, surely, to mourn in silence,
passing that burden onto others.
Wiser counsel prevailed:
I knew her best.
I had written those words.
Just once are we called to fulfil this task.
This was my time; no one else could claim it.
Not to preside over this final paean to her life
seems now unthinkable.

She would have loved the wake.
We drank, we talked, we remembered, we cried.
Younger daughter, she of black humour,
in impromptu speech,
observed how ironic parents should acquire cancers
for bits they no longer needed:
a timely reminder of other mortalities.
Guests, friends, relations drift off,
leaving us alone.
Unprompted, older daughter
voiced sentiments occurring to me too:
in those very earliest days,
unexpected pulses of adrenaline pulled us through;
within the shelter of grief,
a time of excitement, activity,
no room yet in there for depression.
Formalities done, mourners moving on,
worldly goods distributed,

a bleak vista opened up:
how was I – how were we – to live our lives,
to get through the days, let alone the years?
We were saved.
How awful, voiced fellow grievers,
to have this death then, so soon after,
this paralysis of pandemic?
Of course, it wasn't – it was wonderful:
the country closed down,
in state mourning for the passing of this,
one of its best.
Alone, with family, I walked immeasurable distances,
new paths, new ways of surviving;
not forgetting, but remembering;
each step echoing to that ancient rhythm of grief.

A friend of many years loses her partner,
decades younger than mine.
I dare hardly hold the thought.
A mutual contact asks what advice can I give.
Convention dictates stages of grief:
each moving the bereaved forward to a state of acceptance.
Well, mourners should doubt that.
I never denied her death – shockingly evident.
I never bargained. With whom? About what?
I understand anger,
an ever, if diminishing, presence.
Depression too settled on me,
not immediately, but slowly, insidiously.
And as for acceptance, that seems
still a distant,

though perhaps now less elusive, mirage.
Writing, thinking have helped.
I always hoped they would.

Party to an experiment, albeit unwillingly,
it is intriguing to find what does,
what not, trigger grief.
Living in this house, together here for nearly forty years,
causes no pain. Memories infused with her,
leavened by family, friends, time.
A flat, we two its sole residents, wreaks havoc.
In the year after her death, I go just twice,
grateful thanks to others for
excising that deadweight from my world.
Best too to prepare for the unexpected pain
of small things.
I see her presence everywhere;
an inveterate organiser, collector, hoarder,
she filed and tabulated,
useful now for me, a natural pillager.
But to see her writing, that hurts.
Looking at archived messages,
I discover a trail of late texts:
one listing programmes to be recorded,
a sorrow from the ashes.

Many of those admitted to vagaries of grief,
say expect a lifting after first anniversaries.
Wiser minorities talk of two, three years.
Best to fall back on stalest of clichés.
Our lives, our journeys, tell us time does indeed heal.

One day, I will find a freedom,
think of a future beyond comforting confines.
Until then, I shall nurture this grief.
It will not leave unseen.

I Sensed her

Dearest and oldest of friends asks
if I have ever seen her;
no, but one night I sensed her.
Alone, in an old, damp cottage
in a stony, cold village
cascading into grey, murderous, northern seas,
cramped in a creaking bed,
lodged between sleep and dawn,
I felt her hand caress my back:
it will all be well.
Towards the end, alone,
she told me she would always be with me;
her spirit would surround me.
She kept her word.

You and I

You and I,
we learnt together to accept, to live with our lot,
with what we had, no more;
no jealousy ran in our veins.
You and I,
we came to listen – to each other,
to children, to the world.
When enough, we nurtured silence,
learnt the joy of shared peace.
You and I,
we knew how to forget and to forgive
each other, the close;
knew the power that came from pardon,
the grace from letting go,
the charity to turn away.
You and I,
we held the power of humour;
in health, we never stopped laughing –
at ourselves, the near, the curious.
In illness, at death's folly itself,
we faced its absurdities and laughed.
You and I,
we lived through love.
We knew what passion meant, how to love,
how to give, how to share.

We knew how to pace our love, our lives;
love kept our company.
You and I,
read each other perfectly;
we blended so well.
A great match, you said;
I could feel your moods,
sense your change,
find your soul.
You knew every inch of my being,
could tell when to leave, when not.
You summed me up,
you categorised me,
you understood.
I keep, ever remember,
a remark you once made:
I miss you beyond measure, a grief so total.
I miss your charm, your grace, your care,
I miss your being, your acceptance.
I miss you twice-candling each entered church,
one for your soul, one mine.
Most of all, I miss that gentle tread
in the black hour as you wandered around,
sensing your death here,
searching your place beyond.
Nightly I listen for that tread,
soft play on carpeted floors,
echo on wooden.
It's your final gift,
that whispered tread, I miss
more than anything.

You and I, my dear, you and I
we lived,
and we did it so well.

This Sacred Land

Her remaining ashes lay becalmed,
boxed on a book-laden shelf.
Handfuls are scattered in streams,
along known paths, in local haunts;
some reserved for warmer soils.
But I need to go somewhere and mourn,
the two of us together, just us.
Not before sterile casket racks,
but here in this fine ground,
home to shared memories:
black, broken shards piercing carved snow;
Lenten carpeting of yellow flowers;
acres of white blossom blessing longest days;
barren lands bleeding purple treasure.
I love this place more than anywhere.
On a Sunday in the planting season we come,
to glorify her and to remember.
The youngest must now hardly recall,
yet they dig with energy,
help plant a nurtured sapling,
share pouring of ashes,
offer colour in a drab season,
argue, run, hide, shout, laugh,
give life.
I shall come here often,

the two of us together, just us.
I will tie a small blue ribbon to a hidden branch,
known only to the close,
and christen this, your tree.
I see now I must stay here too;
our ashes will mix in a rough, earthen,
turf-topped urn.
My holly will colour your hawthorn in black months;
your confetti-thin blossom soften my thorns.
The view from here is God given,
stretching miles down fretted, contoured valleys
to sunset etched black mountains;
we will never tire of it.
We head a slope falling gently through dead larches, living
rowans,
steepening over rough meadows, hidden boulders,
frayed stands of pine tree,
plunging through noble oak wood
fissured by tumultuous mountain stream,
pouring through cramped straights,
leaping over gritstone towers,
diving beneath stranded trunks,
crashing into collapsing banks,
stilling at crystal pools,
levelling by a martyrs' chapel.
My dear, this place is perfect for us.
The later will come here often
to worship at these sentinel shrines;
and they too will want to rest here.
We will claim a small piece of this sacred land.

I Wish Her Well

This was not supposed to happen;
I never wanted it, looked for it.
I had known her for a while,
thrown together in easy, social play.
We moulded well.
I admired her candour, her smile.
She, I think my generosity of spirit,
laughed at my bad jokes, never silent.
Then death and comforting solitude of pandemic
took me elsewhere to be alone and to grieve.
But she stayed with me, this woman,
a nagging, insistent ache.
A year on – fitting period of mourning –
I proposed a country stroll;
gracious acceptance of this unexpected offer.
The walk was nothing much,
a few hours, sharing ideas, experiences.
I tried to organise other things.
I could see that, in some fashion or other, this might work.
Some skirmishing,
but eventually, as if plucking up courage,
the clearest of messages: this was to go no further.
Lovely man I might be,
but one to be confined to sport, no more.
Somehow reassuring to discover rejection hurts

as much at seventy as seventeen.
But, I reflect, not so surprising;
she much younger,
freed from protracted divorce,
sheltering behind politely constructed reserve;
a sense of mystery,
perhaps shielding a lover.

I still saw her randomly, meeting on courts
and in halls. We chatted amiably.
Nobody would have guessed my torment,
probably not her.
Ill-suited to this walk-on role,
not prepared to play hanger-on,
one treacherously hot afternoon
I walked away, never to return.
A brave decision, the right one;
enduring so much uncontrollable grief,
this pain now fell in my court.
Self-exile hurt more than I ever imagined:
I thought of her constantly,
she awakening in me passions not felt for decades.
Once, picking up children from adjacent field,
I literally trembled at her unseen proximity.

Those few privy to this treason agree:
how awful this should happen so soon.
Give it at least three years. It is not yet two.
But it doesn't work like that.
Things creep up on us, unheard.
We cannot always, and ever,

control our emotions.
One day, she barely figured in my thoughts.
A week later, my head was full of this graceful,
charismatic woman.

I sit in weak, filtered autumnal sun,
waiting a call which will never come,
a text never to arrive,
now nursing two bereavements:
one collective, conventional;
one secretive, shameful.
Shameful because this grief is not right.
How can brief courtside interplay equate with
a relationship safe for over forty years?
But we do not love someone less
because we know less of them,
but because of who they are.
We know, we have been told,
twice nobody dies.
But I know, I am witness:
it is possible, simultaneously,
to grieve for the living,
and for the dead.

I steeled myself:
I would never see her again.
One late autumn afternoon,
weary from dale walking,
returning to the city, car recognised,
I saw her driving towards me,
back to a stony village, face still, quiet.

Through mirrors, I watched
headlights topping each segment
of barrel-vaulted roadside woodland,
candle-like in cathedral nave,
receding red glimmer, blackening void.

It is time. It is far too late.
She has been with me so long;
I wish her well, I really do.

Tears

Where do they all come from?
Why now so many?
For decades, none creased my face;
schooled in tougher climes,
tears were the property of infants,
not adults – certainly not men.

Now I can't stop, every verse bleached white.
Are they for me? Treatment? Fear for a forlorn future?
A long passed youth? For her? A lost love?
An evil world? A poisonous planet? The horror?
I'll never know;
tears come unsourced.

Our parents gave us due warning:
there is nothing wonderful about getting old.
But that it would be so tearful?
I don't recall that message.
So let me pass onto future generations,
lest there be further misunderstanding:
age brings not serenity, but sorrow.

I realise now how towards the end,
this most selfless of women ushered us out,
kept us busy, granted us mundane tasks,

so she could fashion a refuge to house private anguish,
saving the living from that particular horror.
We witnessed only the polite, the conventional.

Dying she told me, once diagnosed,
she had never stopped crying.
I saw so little of that;
I have made up for it since.

Moving On

Bearing Up

However I cut it, it can't be long.
Well past biblical span,
on hearing how well I felt,
consultant recently enthused that men in my condition
were now living fifteen years,
though he stressed, twice, that was exceptional.
I have already had five.
Time to bargain.
Does the count begin from diagnosis
or end of chemo?
Could it now be more than fifteen –
after all, treatment has improved?
What does it matter? It creeps up fast.

Sensible then to plan that funeral service.
She took great care with hers.
Albinoni must take centre stage –
he's always been there –
bookended by Coltrane.
A Love Supreme to gather them in,
that should deter the tepid.
It may be standing room only.
Hers was.
Perhaps Blues Minor,
rapidly to hasten them out.

Useful, with crems so busy these days.
Texts between?
Why not some endings?
Under the circumstances, that seems apt.
Eliot, twice, and Fitzgerald to fill the first void;
the second, Joyce's sublime reflection
on death and grief.
That might work.
It's only a skeleton, of course;
it needs much more thought.
I need to return to it,
but maybe not quite yet.

I love this old, cold house;
I rattle around in it now, choice of five bedrooms.
I pondered moving, a new beginning, new spaces to fill.
A crass idea; she stalks this place,
but so do others. I find it comforting,
we talk often.
Best not to move for at least a year,
convention has it.
Best not to go anywhere, ever;
if you're happy, stay.
I shall die here, or –
I tense at the thought –
neatly to round off this morality play,
in another place nearby.

I sit in a tired, gloomy, book-lined room.
I have spent more of my life here
than in any other place. We shared it for forty years.

Recently others have moved in:
Coltrane lives here now.
Tonight, Nyro and Stills will join him;
they help liven up the place.
This carpet and I have grown old together.
I need a new one.
But is it worthwhile? Will I get value for money?
Actually, I'm rather fond of it. Tricky.
I nurse a glass of appassimento.
I'm drinking too much.
Dear friend asks how I feel about that:
just wonderful.
She overindulged too, savouring New Zealand savs,
well past her best.
I no longer care; my life is not otherwise vice-filled.
I've even given up on cakes.

Outrage and reform,
once so much part of me, are now muted.
I retreat into my own world
of pleasure, and pain.
I have scored that misery
fuelled by illness, death, and grief.
Yet this is not a complete account;
some stories remain untold.
So, having lived through an extraordinary decade
of misfortune, how, you might wonder, are things?
Everything considered, not too bad. Surviving,
bearing up.
I have learnt, again, the comfort of small things,
joy in the world around, unfailing support,

unpredictable pleasures of the young.
I have come too to play more with humour.
Very funny people have shared my journey,
not purveyors of tired, staged jokes, but the witty,
able to construct laughter from the everyday, the banal.
Funniest of all, long dead from my disease,
had an unreal ability to build mansions from the mundane,
holding disparate forces in his head,
teasing out the obscure, moulding the absurd.
We old, we need to laugh. Horrors are to be faced:
illness, death, but, most insidious,
ignorance as to the fate of the young.
Prayer from the old: please let me be the first.

An old friend, least pompous of men,
tells me he has become a better person.
I know precisely what he means.
I have too: more open, accepting, welcoming.
Maybe more generous,
though always careful to avoid suggestions of northern
thrift.
I've used more a modest gift for humour,
enriching my own life too.
She said I laughed at my own jokes;
there are worse failings.
And much more forgiving:
I carry no axes. Forgiveness works.
Why this change?
Because death, grief, loss, minimise everything.
Perhaps too, distanced from duties,
freedom to befriend those I want,

no more, an unexpected pleasure of age.

I've always seen myself as modest,
not one for self-praise, grating vice.
I'm not sure how this has happened,
less whether deserved,
yet now, more than anything, I feel proud.
In diminishing part from conventional prizes –
career, position, legacy, kudos.
In greater, family, close friends.
But mostly for myself.
I have come to own my support,
resident doctor labelling me primary carer –
strange appellation, but true.
Emptying redundant drawers,
unfolding her card,
Christmas, birthday, a milestone of sorts?
I can never thank you enough for all your support,
concern and care.

I cannot deny lodged between grief for the dead
and for the living, cancerous, down –
at times I have lived most
macabre of tearful, gothic nightmares.
Hard to engage, leave, talk, plan.
Days I wanted to retreat, to drink.
But I never have
I'm tougher than I thought
I am so proud I have coped
I'm coming through it
At the corners, I see fingers of light

I can feel it lifting
I have never been so pained
But never so alive
Never lived such vivid colours
Never so aware
I hold firm my empire.

The Great

What is this obsession? Where did it come from?
I never stop thinking about the great.
Do the old come naturally to reflect on magic?
To measure their time?
To use their span to compare?
I am not alone:
glorious poet tells us he thinks constantly
of those who were truly great.
How can we measure greatness?
How can we know?
The greatness of heroism,
not set battles, but individual sacrifice; easier to hold.
A spy, executed, secrets to end a war already revealed;
the young defending a fledging state under a screaming sun;
siblings, barely adult, guillotined resisting a ferocious regime;
an obstinate captain mooring a sea-levelling tanker
in a rapturous harbour, on a beleaguered island.
'Lonely, perhaps, but I doubt many 'impulses of delight'
here.
More bloody-minded determination driven by what?
Fear, duty, creed, indifference to fate?
Whatever it is, at this year end their feats sear through my
head.
Could I have done these things?
And even less delight for others.

I once knew a woman with two sons,
one with an incurable disease,
the other posthumously awarded military honours.
"You must be proud."
"I would rather have him back."

The greatness of creation harder to handle.
How do we know we are there?
Impossible to define, really.
Something to do with the elusive,
the eternal search for the unreachable,
that sense of being elsewhere.
A simplicity, an economy, a lodging in the mind,
an acceptance this sits in another plane,
from opening page, bar, frame,
awareness this is gift wrapped in greatness.
On this year's last day, I log those who
will always be with me. Not many:
both Eliots, Fitzgerald, Forster, Hawks, Coltrane,
Tarkovsky, Keaton, Joyce, Roth.
Is this list now closed?

I have come in this awful year to realise,
too late, the greatness of the ordinary.
To ease pain, deflect depression,
surprising myself, I become a joiner,
aberration for a born sideliner.
Good to meet new people – and it is.
Many aware of this tale
are themselves saddened.
One organiser gathers greatness.

Generosity of spirit, certainly,
skill to predict, to bargain, to moderate.
But more, an ability to live within others,
an extraordinary gift, granted to so few.
He radiates greatness of empathy;
he could lead armies.
Why have I not before grasped this greatness of the
ordinary?
I should have; mighty writers have paved that way.
This can be my one New Year resolution.
A murmuring echo from a new part of me asks:
why not write about it?

Woods

At year-end party time, we gather:
two families, three generations,
eight adults, seven children, two festively-adorned dogs.
We chat, cavort, embrace, drink, eat, remember.
Children food-sated, adults suitably caffeined,
we convoy around these wondrous woods,
edging girdle to this mountainous city.
We annually hold this ritual,
this the second since she died.
Plates are shifting.
Last year wary circling of a sorrowed man:
the close cohort's first bereaved.
This time, I'm involved, I'm central, I'm part of it all,
novelty lost.
Last year, only reverential talk of our dearest lost;
this, ribald, encompassing, fond.
Last year, in sapphire blue she skipped amongst us;
now a grey spectre flits amongst barren trees.
She's moving from sharpest relief to fuzzy heart.
Her life is fading from us.
It is nature's way; it must happen.
There is no other path. We have to move on.
She is going.
As we die, so will her memory slip from this world.
It is all our fates.

Year End

Curtain call on this dreadful year.
Like *The Sopranos* finale,
we come from different places
to land on generous hosts.
Five this time, illness and death depleting roll call.
Never again will we be more than seven.
Sufficient courage to eat,
poignant memories searing deep,
not enough to see in the new.
With an hour to run out,
I leave, walking back along deserted streets,
through whispering woods,
past glittering, illuminated houses,
catching muted, secret celebrations.
An insistent otherness to this empty, eerie, ethereal world:
it is quite ravishingly seductive.
Enchanted, I skip, step and swirl home,
shuffling the women defining this anguished year:
daughters, a dead wife, a lost love.
Time to sleep off this hangover year? Not yet.
That crippling grief is slipping away.
At first hardly feeling this melting,
suddenly an avalanche collapsed.
Celebrations for this newfound liberty:
nothing better than funky '80s soul.

In a cold, candle-black kitchen,
silent, music earpieced,
uninhibited, solitary,
dancing to those addictive sounds,
bending, swaying, turning, smiling,
and bowing.
There is someone I would like you to meet.
You two will, I'm sure, get on well.
Can I introduce: the New Year.

Love Alone Remains

I must write; I have been so saddened
Grief haunted me too long
I had to do something
I had to respond
I couldn't sit vacant
I couldn't let it win
Never before had I written like this
But it came to me one day
That's what I had to do
I could respond
I held a weapon
I could fight
I could write.

I must write; I want to be remembered
I know pride is a cardinal sin
I know this is wrong
I know I shouldn't think this
I know what I would say to fellow sinners
I know this is hypocritical
But I want to die twice
I want the living to say he wrote this.

I must write; I have to
It's a craving, a thirst, a hunger

a lust, an urge
If I resist it will only come back
This passion, this love, this longing
it demands attention
They think I'm listening, I'm involved
They think I'm planning paths, counting contours
They think I'm scheming a slice, tuning a topspin
But I'm not
I'm grappling with demon words
They fill my head
They never leave
It's my drug
I'm addicted
Will I ever come off it?

I must write; I have a secret to pass on
When success palls, vanities fade
Life is a dream, minds wander across oceans
Victories seem pointless
It's easier to live in the past
When you're really sure, totally certain,
absolutely clear
this has all happened
Then
but only then
You will discover
Love alone remains.

Please Forgive Me

This is my memorial to you, my dearest Mary.
I wrote it to assuage grief,
glorify your being, forget another.
I have done my best. You know – you, above all,
really know – how hard I have tried.
I have not succeeded, not fully, on any count.
Yet this must be the end; this is over.

Forgive me, my dear, if these few words
give scant justice to your caring soul;
I have no others.
Forgive me that I am doubly grieved;
it is hard to believe this could have happened
but know I never sought it.
Forgive me if,
in the time left, I see less of you.
I think it best to spend it with the living.
Please forgive me,
but none of this was of my making.

A Tiny Speck

I needed to know.
Months, almost a year,
now, it was safe to go.
I'd seen her there weeks before,
unsure of her reception,
my response,
we'd walked on by.
More determined this time,
more planning, more space.
That stooled,
corner cafe window
an ideal stakeout.
No need, fate.
I saw her immediately.
A brief chat: neutral, polite,
as ever reserved, safe.
Her car packing, late.
A last goodbye,
I turned up towards the café,
blindside waving at her peeping, passing car.
A large black vulture,
on my shoulder for so long,
flew off into the whitest winter sky,
a tiny speck on the horizon.
Someone I knew,

once loved deeply,
drove out of my life.
That final ghost had been laid.
I'm free, it's all over:
poignant, reflective, strangely empty.

Hug Me Close

Anguished year,
hold me tight,
hug me close,
befriend me,
walk with me,
never let me forget.
What a time,
what an amazing time,
what a grieving, desperate, hurting,
wicked, vibrant, chaotic time we two had.
You gifted secrets,
you oozed magic,
you made me tremble,
you left me breathless.
Knowing what I now know,
that pain,
that grief,
given the choice,
would I have lived you?
Yes, of course, yes;
not for all the world,
would I have missed you.
You were extraordinary.
You're the closest friend I've ever had.